SERGEI O. PROKOFIEFF, b
painting and art history at th
encountered anthroposophy in
decision to devote his life to it. He has been active as an author and lecturer since 1982, and in 1991 he co-founded the Anthroposophical Society in Russia. In Easter 2001 he became a member of the Executive Council of the General Anthroposophical Society in Dornach. He is the author of many books, 23 of which have now been published in an English translation.

By the same author:

Anthroposophy and The Philosophy of Freedom
The Cycle of the Seasons and the Seven Liberal Arts
The Cycle of the Year as a Path of Initiation
The East in the Light of the West, Parts One to Three
The Encounter with Evil and its Overcoming through Spiritual Science
The Esoteric Significance of Spiritual Work in Anthroposophical Groups
Eternal Individuality, Towards a Karmic Biography of Novalis
The Foundation Stone Meditation
The Heavenly Sophia and the Living Being Anthroposophia
May Human Beings Hear it!
The Mystery of John the Baptist and John the Evangelist
The Mystery of the Resurrection in the Light of Anthroposophy
The Occult Significance of Forgiveness
Prophecy of the Russian Epic
Relating to Rudolf Steiner
Rudolf Steiner and the Founding of the New Mysteries
Rudolf Steiner's Research into Karma and the Mission of the Anthroposophical Society
The Spiritual Origins of Eastern Europe and the Future Mysteries of the Holy Grail
The Twelve Holy Nights and the Spiritual Hierarchies
What is Anthroposophy?

The Case of Valentin Tomberg
Valentin Tomberg, Rudolf Steiner and Anthroposophy

The Whitsun Impulse
and Christ's Activity in Social Life

SERGEI O. PROKOFIEFF

TEMPLE LODGE

Translated from German by Willoughby Ann Walshe

Temple Lodge Publishing
Hillside House, The Square
Forest Row, RH18 5ES

www.templelodge.com

Published by Temple Lodge 2010

Originally published in German under the title *Der Pfingstimpuls und das Wirken des Christus im Sozialen* by Verlag Freies Geistesleben, Stuttgart, in 2009

© Verlag Freies Geistesleben 2009

This translation © Temple Lodge Publishing 2010

The moral right of the author has been asserted under the Copyright, Designs and Patents Act, 1988

All rights reserved. No part of this publication may be reproduced, stored in a retrieval system, or transmitted, in any form or by any means, electronic, mechanical, photocopying or otherwise, without the prior permission of the publishers

A catalogue record for this book is available from the British Library

ISBN 978 1 906999 15 5

Cover by Andrew Morgan Design
Typeset by DP Photosetting, Neath, West Glamorgan
Printed and bound in Malta by Gutenburg Press

Contents

Preface	vii
1. Renewed Whitsun as Source of Social Forces for the Future	1
Christ's Appearance in the Human Ego	1
Activity of the Christ Impulse in Willing, Feeling and Thinking	5
At the Origin of Esoteric Christianity: the 'Second' Whitsun	7
Initiation Through the Holy Ghost	9
Spiritualization of the Three Soul Forces in Anthroposophy	11
Spiritualization in Social Life as Task of the Anthroposophical Society	12
The Christmas Conference—an 'Inverted' Whitsun	15
Four Stages of Social Development	16
Connection of the Four Social Capabilities with the Four Ether Types	22
Ascent into the Sphere of Social Imaginations	24
2. The Foundation Stone of the Christmas Conference and the Inverted Cult	29
Individual and Social Life	29
Building Stones of the Inverted Cult	30
Cooperation of Spiritual Beings	33
Four Stages of the Inverted Cult	34
Activity of the Angel in the Astral Body	37
Inverted Cult and the Foundation Stone	39
Cultivating the Inverted Cult in a Branch	40
Notes	45
Bibliography	47

Preface

The contents of this book consist of two parts. The first is my report of the lecture I held at Whitsun 2000 on the occasion of the international conference *Development of Anthroposophy in Russia in Light of the Whitsun Festival: Renewed Forces in the Present Human Community*. This conference was organized by the Russian Anthroposophical Society in Moscow.

The second part is dedicated to the theme 'inverted cult', which must be the core of every branch work, in order to become gradually the continuation of the Whitsun event in the present. In this way, both parts are connected internally with each other.

The whole book can be considered as a continuation of my book *The Esoteric Significance of Spiritual Work in Anthroposophical Groups and the Future of the Anthroposophical Society*, also published by Temple Lodge.

I would like to express my heartfelt thanks to Dr Julia Selg and Anna S. Fischer, who each translated part of the initial text from Russian into German.

Dornach, January 2009
Sergei O. Prokofieff

1. Renewed Whitsun as Source of Social Forces for the Future

Christ's Appearance in the Human Ego

The beginning of the second chapter of the Apostle narrative reports about the Whitsun event: when we try to formulate a picture of what happened at that time, we can be amazed at the wonderful precision and depth with which this extremely important event in the development of Christianity is described in the New Testament.

At the beginning we picture the community of the 12 Apostles as representatives of mankind in its past, present, and future spiritual mainstreams. This community is in a state of expectation, having a premonition of a certain important event. The community knows this event can only be consummated on one condition, a condition with which, incidentally, the second chapter of the Apostle narrative begins: 'When the day of Pentecost came, they (the Apostles) were all together in one place' (Acts 2:1, King James version). This is the only preliminary and at the same time extremely important condition for the occurrence of the Holy Ghost's expected outpouring.

The approach of this event is described as blowing, surging wind. We can only understand this picture by remembering that the old Hebrew language expresses 'wind' and 'spirit' with one and the same word (*ruach*). Thus, the Apostles expect the appearance of the Spirit, who heralds Himself as a mighty wind. Then something astounding occurs. Rather than overshadowing the Apostles with just one cloud, which they all receive into themselves, the descending Holy Ghost appears to them as individual tongues of fire. Today we could say as individualized single flames. Each of these little tongues rested on the head of one Apostle. This is an exceptionally meaningful picture: the heavenly flames descend first on the Apostles' heads in order to penetrate through their heads into their hearts. Because of this, there awakens in them a totally new capability: the capability to speak in a special language understandable to every person, to every human heart. This is no external language, not some 'Esperanto', but the original language of the heart, which speaks from soul to soul and therefore is understandable to every being bearing the name 'human'.

Seen as a whole, this has to do with a certain sequence of events. At first an individualization of the Holy Ghost takes place. This consists of everyone receiving his own, inimitable spiritual impulse—his little tongue of spiritual flame—which unites precisely with the organ most strongly individualized in man, with his head. Then the Holy Ghost descends further in a mighty movement from heaven to earth, penetrating and filling the human heart with spiritual fire. Now every Apostle recognizes this Spirit, which he has received individually, which penetrated his heart as the One Spirit. It is the same in all people who have received Him. Thanks to His activity, the Apostles feel themselves united in a new community.

This description given of the Whitsun event enables a crucial passage in the book *The Philosophy of Spiritual Activity* to be better understood. Here we find the first full explanation of individuality in the present epoch of the consciousness soul. Rudolf Steiner relates: 'That's just why a person has my *The Philosophy of Spiritual Activity*, called the philosophy of individuality in the most extreme sense' (GA 212, 7 May 1922). From this unlimited individualism resulted necessarily for Rudolf Steiner the question of how such an extremely individualized person could find himself as free spirit in a new community in the future. As answer to this question the remarkable words appear in *The Philosophy of Spiritual Activity*: 'Only because human individuals *are* one spirit can they also enjoy life side by side. The free person lives in confidence that the other free person belongs with him to a spiritual world and in his intentions will meet with him' (GA 4, Chapter 9; italics Rudolf Steiner). In this communal Spirit, which binds all free people, because according to their being they belong to the same spiritual world, that Whitsun Spirit who had His origin at the time of Christ and later came to full vision at the foundation of the General Anthroposophical Society during the 1923/24 Christmas Conference announces Himself.

Usually the Whitsun event is so understood that through the outpouring of the Holy Ghost something new on the cognition level is disclosed to the Apostles—the Spirit enlightens them, presents them with all-encompassing wisdom. But in reality this event goes much deeper. Not only a new knowledge descends on the Apostles, but through the Holy Ghost's mediation Christ united Himself with their inner being.

In the time of His wanderings through Palestine, the Apostles accompanied Christ at the beginning only in an external manner, for their human consciousness was not yet in a position to comprehend the importance of the event they were witnessing. However, as the central event of the entire earth development, the Mystery of Golgotha, was consummated the Apostles dispersed—except one of whom we will speak specifically later—and none of them could be living eyewitnesses to this mystery. In his lectures devoted to the Fifth Gospel Rudolf Steiner makes us aware that the Apostles' consciousness at that time was increasingly absorbed in a special, dreamlike condition; their spiritual powers were not sufficient to experience this central event of earth evolution in complete alertness (GA 148, 2 October 1913). As a result, the process of distancing themselves from Christ, with whom they wandered three years long through Palestine, continued after the Mystery of Golgotha until it finally culminated in His ascension. Now the Apostles' connection with Christ is broken off for good. There begin the mysterious 10 days between Ascension and Whitsun, which find their culmination in what we can call the new appearance of Christ, but now in the souls of these people.

Here Rudolf Steiner discloses to us an astonishing connection that exists between Christ's appearance and the Holy Ghost's activity in human souls. We can shed light on this connection with the help of the following image. Let us imagine the sun should come right into the midst of mankind. In the physical world the sun is approximately 100 times larger than the earth. When we imagine all its energy, it is immeasurably much stronger than what an earth person can bear. A person cannot remain without protective measures even several kilometres altitude above the earth, because the sun forces are too strong. Now let us imagine that the entire abundance of the sun forces and energies should appear in a single person. Physically such a person would be scorched and exterminated in a thousandth of a second. Something similar, but on the soul-spirit level, would happen with a person in whose soul the divine Christ being would appear. For no single human ego could bear His great cosmic magnitude. Yet we see: people who take up the Christ impulse within themselves do not perish, do not lose their ego, rather—on the contrary—they tread the path to new spiritual development. Here Rudolf Steiner discloses to us the secret why this happens. The reason is that Christ does not appear directly in human souls, but *through mediation* of the being called the Holy Ghost in Christianity (GA 214, 30 July 1922). Thanks to this fact Christ can be present in every human ego without extinguishing it through His great cosmic magnitude. At the same time, He opens for a person truly unforeseen possibilities for individual development.

Thus, we can also say: at Whitsun Christ Himself appeared in the human ego through the Holy Ghost's mediation. Not knowledge about Him, rather His divine being begins to work inside the human soul. As the Apostles go into the world to proclaim to people the holy message of the Resurrected One, of the resurrection, they bring to people not only knowledge of Christ but above all His living force, the force of His presence, however mediated through the Holy Ghost. Henceforth they speak to people about this secret—in the simplest and at the same time most profound language understandable to everyone: the language of the heart.

Rudolf Steiner pointed out many times that Christianity would not have come into being to this day if Christ should have had to wait until He was understood by mankind. But Christ did not wait until people understood Him, but rather appeared Himself, first through the Apostles and then through other people who had united themselves with Him—He appeared directly as living impulse in the whole historical development of mankind. Christ was first active in the human will, which is why these people could perform deeds that seem almost unbelievable to us today when we read the Apostle narrative. This is because at that time He was less active through the cognitive forces of the first Christians, but more so through the forces of much deeper levels of being.

Activity of the Christ Impulse in Willing, Feeling and Thinking

Something quite exceptional occurred regarding the knowledge of Christ. Rudolf Steiner said (GA 182, 16 October 1918) that even the Apostles could only attain a complete understanding of the Mystery of Golgotha and its connection with the entire cosmos approximately 200 to 300 years after their death, when they were in the spiritual world. From the anthroposophical point of view, this opens for us a quite different perspective for understanding the Mystery of Golgotha—an event of such dimension that even the best prepared people require centuries of observation in the spiritual world in order to truly comprehend it. When the Apostles acquired actual understanding they began to inspire from the spiritual world especially suitable people on earth for it. Particularly in the history of early Christianity there are countless examples of how the Apostles and their students inspired people on earth from the highest worlds. Therefore, there occurred in the third, fourth, fifth centuries in the Christian world an amazing striving to *understand* the Mystery of Golgotha. At least one example is mentioned here: the Christian teaching about the Holy Trinity, about the relationship of Christ to the Holy Trinity. In this teaching we have such astonishingly fine conceptions as 'not reduced to one and indivisible' or 'born, but not created'. In the Gospels we do not find such an elaborate teaching about the Holy Trinity. This is because the Trinity teaching stems from the inspirations of the above-mentioned Apostles, who as they had grasped the entire cosmic extent of the Mystery of Golgotha in the spiritual world went on in the following centuries to inspire the best prepared people, who took the path of Christian initiation. In the works of very early Church fathers we discover traces of their inspiration.

But the development of Christianity goes further. During the first centuries of the Christian age the Christ impulse was more active in human willing. Christ appeared from the eleventh, twelfth, thirteenth centuries in the area of human feeling. In this connection we look at a figure like Francis of Assisi. In him we have a person whose soul was totally penetrated by the Christ impulse and who therefore saw Christ in all suffering people, even in the most outcast among them, the lepers. When we learn about Francis of Assisi (1182–1226) with his sympathy, his love that could even heal people, we begin to sense the enormous depth and unlimited possibilities of Christ-filled feeling which occurred at that time. Or let's take an example from a later time. (Under the special spiritual historical conditions of Russia earlier development stages still persist in later times.) Let's look at the great St Seraphim of Sarov (1759–1833), about whom Rudolf Steiner in conversation with Margarita Voloschin said that in him one of the greatest individualities of mankind was incarnated, who however in this incarnation as Seraphim of Sarov had taken upon himself the task of working in mankind through the feeling sphere, through sympathy.

From anthroposophy it is known that we currently live in the age of the consciousness soul as well as in a time that is guided by a new time spirit—Michael. Furthermore, in earth development the dark age of Kali Yuga ended in the year 1899. Today we are going through a quite special spiritual historical constellation. As a result, the central Christian impulse, first active in willing and then in feeling, had to appear gradually in human consciousness. That means we, instead of remaining more or less ignorant followers of Christ (as just believers), should henceforth become *knowers*. Or in order to express this new situation in words of the Gospel, from God's servants we should gradually become His friends (John 15:15), know the plan of the divine world structure, including all laws of development, human goals and tasks, and much more of which anthroposophy relates to us. Then thanks to anthroposophy we gradually can become *conscious* co-workers of Christ participating in the tasks of leading mankind. In other words, something new must make the general development of Christianity fruitful in our time. This can only come out of the source of esoteric Christianity, whose representative is anthroposophy.

At the Origin of Esoteric Christianity: the 'Second' Whitsun

If a person follows the emergence of esoteric Christianity back to the time of Christ, one can actually find the moment when it was founded. This happened as a result of a special event related to the Whitsun impulse. When we become familiar with the Holy Script, we can discover: the Holy Ghost's descent is not only related in the Apostle narrative, but also in the penultimate chapter of the most esoteric of the Gospels, the Gospel of St John. It points out the mission of the Holy Ghost did not occur initially 50 days after the Mystery of Golgotha, but as early as the first Easter, immediately after Christ's ascension. Regarding this Gospel citation I would like to say this event is of immeasurable importance for the following earth development: 'Then the same day at evening, being the first day of the week, when the doors were shut where the disciples were assembled for fear of the Jews, came Jesus and stood in the midst, and saith unto them, Peace be unto you. And when he had so said, he shewed unto them his hands and his side. Then were the disciples glad, when they saw the Lord. Then said Jesus to them again, Peace be unto you: as my Father hath sent me, even so send I you. And when he had said this, he breathed on them, and saith unto them, Receive ye the Holy Ghost' (John 20:19–22, King James version).

For the entire event there are two Whitsuns—one happening on the fiftieth day after the Mystery of Golgotha, which is known to the entire Christian world, and the second (chronologically the first), an esoteric Whitsun, which occurred on the evening of the day Christ consummated the ascension. Here a person must inevitably ask: why do we find the information about *this* Whitsun only in the Gospel of St John? The reason is that evangelist John was *the only one* among Christ's Apostles who experienced this first Whitsun with full consciousness and therefore could report about it in his Gospel. All the other Apostles still had to wait a full 50 days before the Holy Ghost's overshadowing could be granted to them too. In this first and original Whitsun, which was received in full consciousness by only one of the Apostles—evangelist and apocalyptist John—we have the origin of that Christianity which since that time has been called esoteric.

According to Rudolf Steiner's spiritual research John is the same individual initiated by Jesus in the person of Lazarus in Bethany. The connection between these two individualities is expressed in an especially delicate way in the Gospels, where Christ spoke just twice about the Apostle closest to Him whom He *loved*. He 'loved' Lazarus and He loved the author of St John's Gospel. In this connection Rudolf Steiner reveals to us a deep truth: it actually is a case of one and the same individuality!

Through the first Christian initiation consummated by Christ Himself, Lazarus, who became John as Christ Jesus' 'beloved Apostle', was the only conscious witness of the Mystery of Golgotha. Along with Mary, mother of Jesus and earthly bearer of the divine Sophia forces (see GA 100, 25 November 1907), he represented all Apostles—and through them all of humanity—under the cross on Golgotha. This makes his person worthy of the Whitsun event—not like the other Apostles after 50 days, but directly on the day of Christ's ascension—and allows him to become the founder of esoteric Christianity. We know: the Gospel of St John written by this Apostle was for many generations of mystics and saints a real book of initiation. Its lists seven stages of initiation—washing the feet, being taken hostage, crowning with thorns, bearing the cross, experiencing mystical death, being laid in the grave, and transforming through ascension. Thousands of initiates and mystics, whose names to a great extent have not been preserved by external history, have passed through these stages in the course of centuries. For them the Gospel of St John was practical guidance on one of the two main paths of Christian initiation.

Initiation through the Holy Ghost

Belonging to the essence of the second Christian initiation path is the second book written by evangelist John: the 'Apocalypse'. Rudolf Steiner called it an 'initiation book' (GA 104). There is no contradiction that it also describes events of the future. For in the process of initiation a person overtakes earth evolution and becomes spiritual witness to future events. This second path of Christian initiation lived on in the circles of true Rosicrucians. Therefore, when Rudolf Steiner organized for the first time on Trinity Sunday* 1907 in Munich a congress for the German Section of the Theosophical Society (whose General Secretary he was at that time), it was a real Rosicrucian congress in which the first impulses for a new Rosicrucian art were also given. As is known, the hall in which this congress met was especially decorated with the seven apocalyptic seals. In them scenes from the Apocalypse were represented in pictorial, imaginative form. In their arrangement these scenes expressed the seven basic stages of Christian-Rosicrucian initiation, which Rudolf Steiner later described explicitly in the book *An Outline of Occult Science*.

As of the thirteenth century, before the Rosicrucians became its main bearers (see GA 130, 27 September 1911), esoteric Christianity lived in the West in the form of the Grail mystery. In this mystery the experience of the Holy Ghost was the central moment of divine service, which the knights performed in the Grail castle: the appearance of the Spirit in the image of a dove above the holy chalice. The experience of the Holy Ghost was also the central point of Rosicrucian initiation. Therefore Rudolf Steiner called it an initiation through the Holy Ghost (see GA 131, 5 October 1911), which encompassed the whole person. In our time this stream continues in anthroposophy. In it esoteric Christianity or the Christianity of the Holy Ghost appears for the first time on the plane of external history. Its main task remains, as already men-

---

*In the Eastern Christian church, Trinity Sunday is the same day as Whitsunday, whereas in the Western church it is a week later. The 1907 Congress began on a Whitsunday, according to the Western Christian calendar.

tioned, to enable Christianity—and actually Christ Himself, who accompanies mankind's history since the Mystery of Golgotha—to appear as a higher, supersensible reality in our daily waking consciousness. In order for this to occur, we must first familiarize ourselves with the Christ being as well as His activity in the cosmos, on earth, and in humans through deep understanding. This Christ knowledge from the source of esoteric Christianity, whose roots we have just followed, will in our time become the possession of all mankind thanks to anthroposophy. Therefore, Rudolf Steiner called anthroposophy the new spiritual language in which present-day mankind can learn to speak with Christ (see GA 175, 6 February 1914).

However, what anthroposophy represents for us to begin with as only knowledge was for its founder real spiritual experience. Anthroposophy came into the world because there was in the present epoch a man who, proceeding from the forces of the consciousness soul, could meet Christ in the spiritual world and experience Him *in full consciousness*—on the highest level of supersensible knowledge (Intuition). This man was Rudolf Steiner.

In view of the 350 volumes of Rudolf Steiner's entire publications we realize with amazement: their total contents cover the results of his spiritual research, which fill thousands of pages. About his individual personal experiences in the spiritual world, however, he devoted merely a few lines in his autobiography as well as several places in his lectures. How much his behaviour differs from the general tendency today to write immediately about one's own supersensible experiences without noticing thereby how one really allows oneself to be guided by concealed egotism. In contrast to this Rudolf Steiner almost never speaks about his own experiences, but solely about the results of the objective spiritual research conducted by him. Certainly, he cannot silently pass over the central spiritual event of his initiation in the description of his life. But he mentions it only very briefly and devotes merely a few lines to it. The talk is of a 'knowledge festival', whose central point was 'having stood before the Mystery of Golgotha', which Rudolf Steiner went through around the turn of the century (GA 28, Chapter 26). For him this event meant a spiritual experience: consciously taking up within himself the Christ impulse through mediation of the Holy Ghost.

Spiritualization of the Three Soul Forces in Anthroposophy

From then on Rudolf Steiner described again and again, albeit in fully objective, spiritual-scientific form, the Holy Ghost's activity in man. What happens when the human soul is filled with the Holy Ghost? Then a real wonder occurs: all material being around him, all that upon which his glance falls, which his hand touches, is filled with Spirit. All material becomes a revelation of the spiritual. For this is the true Whitsun wonder! All material becomes everywhere quasi-translucent and the Spirit begins to speak through it.

But what did Rudolf Steiner do with this revelation? Out of this spiritual experience he wrote his most important book, which—according to his own words—contains the outline of all anthroposophy.[1] This book is the above-mentioned *An Outline of Occult Science* with its magnificent image of world evolution, which was looked upon with consciousness penetrated by the Holy Ghost. For when the Holy Ghost begins to work in a person's consciousness, then for this person the entire world evolution—which we otherwise only know in its material form as currently represented in the theory of Darwin and Haeckel—is all at once filled with Spirit and spiritual beings, hierarchies creating and penetrating the entire universe with their being, who begin to speak to him through all its events. In the middle of the entire world structure *one* central figure is recognizable—Christ as Sun Logos, as well as His most essential activity on earth, the Mystery of Golgotha.

For all its profound spiritual content, *An Outline of Occult Science* is however formulated in contemporary, strictly intellectual-scientific form. This is a splendid example of what happens when the spirit penetrates human thinking. Therefore, following the thoughts of this book allows the reader to come into touch with the activity of the Spirit beyond the world of external sense perception, which means taking up the Spirit in oneself. Transformation of human cognitive faculties through the Holy Ghost's impulse—this is how we can characterize the effect of this book on us.

The next stage of development described was achieved a few years after the appearance of this book (in 1910). In autumn 1913, the foundation stone was laid on which the first Goetheanum was erected. What is this building? Actually, it represents exactly the same *Outline of Occult Science*, but now become visible in the imaginative forms of the Goetheanum or 'Johannes Building', as it was originally called. In this building various types of fine arts have been renewed and transformed from the source of the Holy Ghost.

Thus, we can say: at the beginning of anthroposophy's development process on earth the *cognitive forces* were spiritualized in order to make it possible for us to tread the modern Christian initiation path; then the *feeling forces* were spiritualized through the means of a new art; and finally through spiritualized *will forces* various practical areas were fructified—medicine, science, education, therapeutic pedagogy, the area of religion (Christian Community), agriculture, and many more.

Spiritualization in Social Life as Task of the Anthroposophical Society

The culmination of this development is finally the question of spiritualization and transformation of the human social sphere. How can social life become bearer of the Christ impulse? How can Christ Himself, who henceforth works into mankind in etheric form, appear directly in human social life? This extremely important question for our time can be formulated like this: how can people who tread the modern spiritual training path—the anthroposophical initiation path—prepare with their group activity the spiritual space in which the etheric Christ can appear in order to work within human social connections?

The possibility for this was brought about by Rudolf Steiner at the Christmas Conference. In other contexts various aspects of this event have already been treated.[2] Here this theme shall be illuminated from another side. The focal point of the Christmas Conference is creating the spiritual foundation stone, which Rudolf Steiner consequently gave to the members of the Anthroposophical Society as the supersensible basis for the new Michael community. This foundation stone—surrounded like a spiritual veil by the Foundation Stone Meditation expressing its being through the word—is nevertheless independent of this a spiritual reality for itself, a reality of the etheric world. Therefore, a person can—according to Rudolf Steiner's words—at that moment when he really so desires lay the spiritual foundation stone in his heart, naturally not in the physical heart, but in the etheric heart.

From Rudolf Steiner's spiritual research we know the wonderful, profound Christian mystery connected with the human heart.[3] In it the process of etherizing the human blood is carried out continually. The blood stops existing materially in the human heart and rises as etheric stream from heart to head. In this connection Rudolf Steiner refers to the spiritual-scientific fact that, since the Mystery of Golgotha, parallel to this stream—the microcosmic stream of the etherized human blood, which flows from heart to head—a second macrocosmic stream rises in the same direction from heart to head, as the stream of Christ's etherized blood. This Christ stream is present in every heart independent of whether a person is Christian in his daily consciousness or not. These two streams, the microcosmic and macrocosmic, run parallel in present-day humans and do not touch each other at first. Therefore, one of the most important tasks in our epoch is consciously uniting them. Rudolf Steiner says that people who succeed in uniting them in their hearts will be in a position to perceive Christ in the etheric vicinity of the earth.

When we look at the foundation stone and its meditative mantric expression from this point of view, we discover that both have microcosmic and macrocosmic components. If we actually submerge this double foundation stone in the depths of our ether heart, where this central Christian mystery occurs, we will discover how this foundation stone presents to us a real path for uniting both etheric streams in our heart. Then we experience spiritually the foundation stone having this double microcosmic/macrocosmic nature, because once submerged in the human heart it becomes a bridge uniting both streams of etherized blood. The foundation stone transforms itself in a concrete path leading to the experience of the etheric Christ.

While Rudolf Steiner entrusted this foundation stone to the members of the Anthroposophical Society at the Christmas Conference, he emphasized particularly that in their hearts it was not simply the basis for their own individual development but above all the foundation stone for a new human community. Therefore, Rudolf Steiner realized with us the Gospel word, mentioned frequently in his lectures: 'My kingdom is not of this world' (John 18:36, King James version). He explains it thus: 'The kingdom of Christ Jesus is not of this world, but it must be active in this world, and human souls must be the tools of the kingdom which is not of this world' (GA 175, 6 February 1917). In other words: Christ came into this world in order to found His kingdom in its midst where the illegitimate ruler of this world, Ahriman, prevails.

Precisely this is the esoteric task placed before the Anthroposophical Society at the Christmas Conference: to be a fully open society, undifferentiated from the external world, but sharing its destiny completely—and at the same time to be a society that stands on the spiritual foundation stone, which does not stem from this world where Ahriman the Ruler of Darkness prevails, but which is produced directly from Christ's realm. From Christ's kingdom stems that foundation stone laid in the hearts of people by Rudolf Steiner, whose wish it was to found the new human community he named the 'General Anthroposophical Society' at the Christmas Conference. Since then the basic esoteric task of this community remains presenting to mankind for the future a prototype of what a real Christian community is. In the future a human community can only be called Christian when it incorporates in full measure this spiritual principle. Then it will be a community that doesn't flee from the world into a cloister—or into an ashram—but remains in the midst of the contemporary ahrimanic civilization and continues, in the Michaelic sense, the fight to master those tasks placed before us today for furthering mankind's development. Nevertheless, such a community that dwells in the realm of the 'Rulers of the World' stands imperturbably on the foundation stone, which is not of this world, but from Christ's kingdom. In all coming times this must become the *new community-building principle* for people. All anthroposophists are called upon, when they so desire, to become the first community in mankind wishing to realize profound social Christian principles in its midst.

The Christmas Conference—an 'Inverted' Whitsun

Everything represented here has a direct connection to the being of the Whitsun festival. On 25 December 1923, Rudolf Steiner, referring to the Holy Ghost's appearance, completed the process of laying the foundation stone in the thought light surrounding it in the spiritual world (see GA 260, 25 December 1923). With it Rudolf Steiner shows how the Christmas Conference event is placed in the stream of esoteric Christianity, namely as continuation and further development of the Grail on the one hand and the Rosicrucian stream on the other hand. Central to the Grail mysteries the Holy Ghost appears above the Grail chalice each year on Good Friday. Rudolf Steiner called the Rosicrucian initiation a 'Spirit initiation' (GA 131, 5 October 1911), which means an initiation filling a person with the Holy Ghost. In this way both main streams of esoteric Christianity were united with the Whitsun impulse.

Through the appearance of the Holy Ghost in the foundation stone's aura we have further allusion to what the Christmas Conference means in the process of mankind's mystery evolution. It is not only a renewal of the original Whitsun, but also its further metamorphosis.

In the stream of the New Mysteries, the Christmas Conference represents an 'inverted' Whitsun. This follows in all clarity from the character of the foundation stone itself as well as the meditation connected with it. In the imagination of the original Whitsun event, with which we began this observation, the Spirit descends from the heights while first penetrating human heads and then dipping further down to speak out of human hearts.

However, by 'inverted' Whitsun we have the opposite process. Here in the human heart is laid the supersensible foundation stone, which bears the impulse of the Holy Ghost in its aura. From the depths of the heart this Spirit rises to the head where it will be borne henceforth with consciousness into the world. Therefore, in the fourth part of the meditation the direction from heart to head, in which the Spirit ascends in man, is emphasized three times. When the Spirit comes to light in the head, that is in the forces of our individual consciousness, the task of carrying this Spirit's impulse into the whole of earth evolution awakens in us. This is only possible when we are capable of standing imperturbably on that foundation stone, the *Stone of Love* (see GA 260, 25 December 1923). As such a Stone of Love it also becomes the foundation stone of the New Jerusalem, which represents the future Jupiter cosmos—the future Cosmos of Love (see GA 11 and GA 104).

In this way there arises before our eyes a totally new development perspective, in which the individual and social principles are united harmoniously. Laying the foundation stone in one's own heart can only be consummated by a person in an individual way. Nobody is able to do it for another person. When this has occurred, when a person has laid it in his own heart, based on his own, pure individual cognitive forces, it begins to work in his heart and becomes the foundation stone for a new human community, which in the sense of the New Mysteries can be called a Christian community and which unites a person directly with Christ's activity in the etheric world.

Four Stages of Social Development

At various places in his lectures Rudolf Steiner describes this process in more detail. Here we will turn to one of these descriptions in which he specifies a series of social development stages through which mankind must proceed in order that the 'inverted' Whitsun, which from now on progresses from a person, who has become a free and conscious bearer of the Spirit, can become reality in human social life. In this connection, Rudolf Steiner speaks about four stages whose complete realization in mankind's development will take several thousand years. Disregarding that it will require such a long time to reach this goal, people must be conscious today of this new task and set out on the concrete path to its realization—through forming communities that strive to develop inner qualities connected with the 'inverted' Whitsun. We know the future will never come if it is not prepared early, albeit in very small circles. That is the principle of the true esoteric. What is initially prepared in small circles will later become the possession of all people. Therefore, we do that about which we speak not for the sake of ourselves, but for the sake of all mankind. One can compare this with laying the foundation stone in one's own heart, which we do not consummate for the sake of our own personal development but for the sake of founding a new human community in which the future should be prepared.

About which social qualities or social experiences—that are in my opinion connected directly with the realization of the 'inverted' Whitsun—does Rudolf Steiner speak? Principally, he points out the indispensability of strengthening one's own interest in his fellow men. In lectures he stresses more than once that it would be better not to speak at first about human love, because love is something lofty and extremely difficult, but one should simply begin with a sincere interest in the other person. (Here I would like to emphasize especially that we should not confuse love with the usual feeling of sympathy or affection, which happens very often in our time. Because people generally don't know what true spiritual love is, they easily confuse it with their own feelings and emotions.) How often can we observe: a person speaks in nice words about brotherly love and overlooks at the same time the person who sits next to him. The concrete person does not interest him, because such an abstract idealist is only filled with love for mankind as a whole, which means for nobody. On the contrary, Christ spoke about the least among us!

In this sense, Rudolf Steiner speaks about interest in the concrete person, for there lies the first stage in creating a new social reality on the etheric plane. Just begin not simply with ordinary interest, but with such that can grow out of inner meditation and that allows us to perceive *in pictorial form* the concrete person standing before us. Here Rudolf Steiner alludes to the exceptionally great importance of art. He says: what does art ultimately serve, above all renewed art from anthroposophical sources? It serves the *discovery of man*. Not a cold, dissecting-intellectual form, but human knowledge in imaginative form in which a person becomes a living picture for another person. In Russia one would say: then one person becomes for the other an icon, man's spiritual core being, through whom the spiritual world shines. When we learn with all of the awareness available to us to perceive a person's slightest remark with burning soulful interest, to observe his gestures, facial expression, mimicry, movements, etc., all this becomes—when we develop an artistic sense—an image, a revelation of his true being which is the eternal in each person.[4]

Consequently, through such a pictorial experience of the other person—achieved through the force of our meditations—every person is for us exceptionally interesting and quite special, because every human personality is infinitely fascinating and individual. But that is not all. In order to realize this capability on the social level we must take a further step. It is necessary to learn to grasp how this eternal human being, revealing to us its pictorial nature, exercises on us an effect which one can compare with the sensation of warmth or cold. The one person we perceive in pictorial form 'becomes warm to one, another person makes one cold' (GA 185, 26 October 1918). In this connection Rudolf Steiner points to a detail that is especially important. He says: 'Worst of all are the people who make one neither warm nor cold' (ibid.), because such people's souls are in the process of dying away.

Thus the first stage of realizing this etheric reality in the social area (about which we will speak later) encompasses developing such an intensive interest in one's fellow man that his pictorial nature becomes transparent, and in company with him the observer can be presented with warmth or cold. That is the first stage. Rudolf Steiner says that a person will need until the end of the current fifth post-Atlantean cultural epoch to completely develop this special capability.

The second quality is connected with language. We must get to know entirely anew how a person speaks, penetrate the external form of his language (here Eurythmy can be especially helpful) and experience language through another person's words as true revelation of his soul.[5] For this one must develop in oneself an entirely new capability, namely being able to perceive that *what* a person says is not as important as *who* says it.

Rudolf Steiner mentioned many times one characteristic example in this connection. He speaks about two individualities. One was the outstanding German author at the end of the nineteenth century, Herman Grimm (1828–1901). The other was a personality who in the history of the twentieth century played a fateful, one could even say fatal, role. We're talking about Woodrow Wilson (1856–1924), the American president in the 1920s, who disseminated in the whole world the famous 14 points regarding self-determination of nations and folk, which to this day continues to work in the most remote regions of the earth and often causes wars and bloody ethnic conflicts. In this connection, Rudolf Steiner said: 'It is possible to take over certain sentences from Woodrow Wilson and place them in articles by Herman Grimm, for they almost sound like Herman Grimm's sentences and articles' (GA 185, 26 October 1918). Both wrote articles containing words and sentences that when compared with one another are almost the same word for word. Where does the difference exist? It is a matter of *who* is speaking in each case. The words can be good and right, but if the one who expresses them does not live in them, does not penetrate them with his individual ego, then things basically right in and of themselves can develop destructive forces in the world.

Rudolf Steiner emphasizes that by living internally, spiritually in language on the second stage we must learn to differentiate from what source a person speaks. He points to Herman Grimm, who speaks out of his entire human personality, which is why his words are the result of great inner work and spiritual struggle—the struggle of an individual human ego seeking truth and knowledge. By contrast Woodrow Wilson, who uses nearly the same words, is in his subconsciousness possessed by an ahrimanic demon, who speaks through him (see ibid.). The human personality hardly participates in the process.

This will be the special task of the future sixth cultural epoch: not allowing oneself to be diverted by *what* a person says, not to be addicted to his nice words, not even when he takes them from anthroposophy, but to ask oneself persistently: what sort of person is the one who speaks these words? Does his human personality stand behind the truths he expresses—or not? If the person does not stand behind them—no matter how lovely the presentation may be—then they are only empty words and according to Apostle Paul a 'tinkling cymbal' (I Corithians 13:1, King James version). Such words bear no spiritual reality. No living spirit is present in them.

Further, Rudolf Steiner says that as we listen to other people's language we can in the future develop in us the capability of observing them to the extent that we internally gradually begin to perceive various colours through their words—that the *manner in which* a person speaks will be accompanied in our souls by an experience of colour sensations. Then many statements and even single words will produce the sensation for example of the colour red, others the colour blue, and so forth. With Eurythmy and also through speech formation (*Sprachgestaltung*) we can achieve today an initial experience in this sense. In the lecture mentioned, Rudolf Steiner says in this regard that mankind will require a still longer period for developing this second capability. Therefore, mankind will not yet have been able to achieve its complete development during the fifth post-Atlantean cultural epoch. For this also the sixth epoch or at least part of it will be required.

The third capability we have to develop consists of witnessing other people's life so intensively and spiritually that the effect is absorbed in our breathing. A wonderful image! We must learn to inhale and exhale other people. 'People will have to breathe one another in the area of feeling' (ibid.). Just imagine what an intimate connection there will be between people. In our time such witnessing is generally known only in negative form. When someone near us has a fit of rage, perhaps our heart begins to beat faster and our breathing rhythm changes. Positive experiences in this area are much less entrusted to us. But the latter is what must be developed. When we meet a person, precisely our inner breathing informs us something about his soul condition. Perhaps through intercourse with him our breathing becomes more harmonic and freer, or to the contrary—we experience impeded breathing, perhaps even shortness of breath. Through all this we will in the future be able to clearly judge another person's moral condition. Indeed for developing this capability the entire sixth cultural epoch will be required.

The fourth and greatest capability leads people still further, which Rudolf Steiner expresses in a paradoxical manner. Every person today can already perceive this in rudimentary form, even if often from a quite difficult perspective. For at this fourth stage Rudolf Steiner says we must learn to digest each other. 'People will have to digest each other in the area of willing' (ibid.). This means we will have to learn to experience more consciously the karma that connects us with other people. This karma appears in us initially as a difficult-to-digest stone, which lies on our path and over which we continually stumble in social relationships with other people. For we seek in others the person, but bump the whole time against his 'Double' (*Doppelgänger*) and often do not account for the fact that we ourselves are guilty. Such a stone of difficult-to-digest karma from the past must be digested by us—that means, be transformed into positive, constructive elements of our common destiny. The basic problem here is that we do not move such a karmic 'stone', cannot simply throw it away; we can only change it inwardly. Precisely that will be the most important task of the future spiritual community: to work on transforming karma. In order to realize this task mankind needs even more time. A greater part of the seventh cultural epoch will be necessary for this. Although we, as it seems, still have before us a lot of time for consciously developing these qualities it is however imperative that we begin with it today. For this anthroposophy has been given to us. The solution of our social problems depends directly on the fact that these capabilities exist in people, if only in initial germinal form.

It goes without saying these qualities cannot be developed by studying Rudolf Steiner lectures and books alone at home. Their complete development cannot even be achieved in a small group that is enthusiastic about the idea. We can only realize them to full extent in a social community as is provided in the anthroposophical world society in which we have the possibility of meeting a wide variety of people who differ not only in age, mentality and character, but also stem from various folks and cultures. With these otherwise very different people, who certainly strive for anthroposophical knowledge, we can best tackle the development of the qualities described.

Thus, we must learn to experience other people in their pictorial nature to the point of perceiving the warmth or cold emanating from them. We must learn to listen to their language, to perceive the individual colour determination of their souls through their words. Also we must acquire the capability of inhaling and exhaling other people. Finally we need the courage not to run away from all difficulties that arise today in a growing social community. Despite everything we must become co-workers of Christ in the field of karma and develop in this field inner, pure Michaelic forces that allow us gradually to 'digest' this karma, because there is really no other way to found true Christian community on earth.

Connection of the Four Social Capabilities with the Four Ether Types

In an attempt to summarize the four stages described, we can observe how their being in the social sphere relates to the concrete work with the four ether forces. This is the next stage that must be realized by mankind based on experiencing mutual social contacts on the physical plane and, eventually, the etheric plane.

For when we feel that a person radiates in his pictorial nature warmth or cold, we experience on the social plane an activity of the warmth ether. If we perceive through language a person's manifold soul colouring, then we experience the light ether on the social plane.

When we learn to breathe so that we receive in our breathing another person's soul being, that is receive him where the chemical forces of our organization are concentrated, then we enter into the activity sphere of the next higher ether type. In the present time we are still beings who inhale oxygen, which is life, and exhale carbon dioxide, which bears death. From spiritual science we know the most important task of the future is learning to perfect consciously what the plants do for us today: take in death, inhale poisonous material, and breathe out life, exhale health. On the third stage described this process must be accomplished primarily on the social level. This will be the realization of the basic Manichaean principle, which is a person learning with time to take in or 'inhale' social evil and 'exhale' good, thereby working with the chemical or tone ether on the social plane.

When we finally dip down into our circulatory system, that is in our own depths where the karma of the past is active in us (for we bear it in our circulation-limb* system), in order to work with this foundation in social life we must learn to transform it by means of life ether forces.

Thereby we gradually create in the social sphere the 'space' in which the etheric Christ can appear, for He will never appear again on the physical plane. We know the greatest aberrance of today's occultism exists in expecting Christ here or there in a physical body.[6] In reality, since the Mystery of Golgotha, Christ is no longer physical, rather He is present supersensibly in mankind and henceforth active among people in a new, etheric form (see GA 118).

As God of the human ego, Christ is especially connected with every individual person. Beginning in our time and becoming even

---

*Alternatively translatable as 'metabolic-limb' system. (Editor's note.)

stronger in the sixth cultural epoch He will be increasingly active in etheric form as well as in social relations of people among one another. However, a person must create the corresponding conditions for His activity in the social sphere—or the etheric 'space', which out of socially active forces consists of warmth, light, chemical and life ethers. Through human social cooperation there can gradually come into being that social-etheric sphere in which the etheric Christ can appear.

At this place one may ask: who possesses this knowledge except for anthroposophists? Who besides them presently has the possibility of really treading this path in full consciousness? Therein also lies our great responsibility as anthroposophists compared with the whole of future mankind, whereby it concerns not only an individual responsibility but also one borne by people who strive to form a completely new human community in which the etheric Christ can become active one day.

Ascent into the Sphere of Social Imagination

At the end let's look once again at the first stage: experiencing the pictorial nature of people. This stage is especially important, because it will be achieved in the near future and we do not have much more time remaining for its realization. Without this all of the following stages cannot be perfected in the right way. Therefore, in other lectures, Rudolf Steiner describes this stage in great detail and calls it the awakening to the soul-spirit of other people (see GA 257, 27 February 1923).

What does such an inner awakening mean? It is the ascent of our consciousness to a higher stage than our awakening every morning. In sleep we are in the world of dreams and awaken out of it into our fresh daily consciousness. What is now necessary is that we achieve in the social sphere the next level, which is *beyond* normal daily human consciousness. By experiencing other people pictorially in that we receive the revelation of their soul-spirit being we must, starting from our ordinary consciousness (in which we all too often use cold, critical and judgemental thinking concerning our fellow human beings), ascend to a higher stage—that of pure *imaginative* experience of other people. If we succeed in this first stage, we will observe that in contrast to abstract thinking, which only analyses and divides, this higher imaginative thinking—or heart thinking—works in us as a new organ of perception in a unifying, social manner.

Rudolf Steiner called the ascent of human consciousness into the sphere of social imagination the 'inverted' cult,[7] which leads us directly into the above-mentioned higher mystery of the 'inverted' Whitsun, for the 'inverted cult' is its most important component. As a result, a person receives through interest in the spiritual, in another person's eternal self, the possibility to *awaken* to pure, imaginative perception as the basis for completely new social relationships. This decisive step is indispensable in our time for establishing a Christian community in mankind for the future.

If we really want to *understand* social life, we should not belittle the importance of thinking, which plays a role thereby. An understanding of social legality is actually achievable only with its help. If, however, we want to *accomplish* something in this social sphere and this task approaches us only through our cognitive forces, we will very soon find that naked, judgemental thinking works disconnectedly in social fulfilment and thereby calls forth only antisocial processes. As a result, people begin to split into parties, to defend different viewpoints, and everyone begins to represent dogmatically only his own 'truth', which then becomes idealized so that in the end all social relationships are destroyed. If we raise ourselves, however, through a real interest in the other person—which leads to inner awakening and thereby observing his soul-spirit foundation on a higher, imaginative stage—we understand all true social life can only be realized in the manner suggested. Intellectual understanding is just the initial step upon which follows the work guided ever more out of social imaginations. Only with its help can a new, dignified social life be founded in mankind.

Connected with what has been said is the most important spiritual event of our time: Christ's appearance in etheric form. We ascend from the path described to the sphere of Imagination, as social community in those spheres where the etheric Christ is active today and an encounter with Him can happen not only as individual experience of a single human personality but becomes a *community experience*. Rudolf Steiner points to this astounding ideal when he says Christ will appear in gatherings of people and speak to them His word. 'It may today seem grotesque but it is nevertheless true that sometimes when people sit together, without anyone knowing it, and also when larger numbers of people gather and wait, they will see the etheric Christ! There He will be, will deliberate, will cast His word into gatherings. We are absolutely approaching these times' (GA 130, 1 October 1911). So this can happen in social life out of 'inverted' Whitsun forces; a new etheric 'space' must be created, which means there must come into being a special spiritual sphere in which Christ can appear to people as well as in social life.

Rudolf Steiner says the current fifth post-Atlantean epoch is the period for developing the consciousness soul, in which the human individual ego shall attain its highest unfolding. In reality this highest stage of developing the individual ego, which in our time is exclusively one's own responsibility, may in no event be bypassed. Here Rudolf Steiner points out the further task of the consciousness soul will be to attain its future transformation into the imaginative soul (see GA 145, 29 March 1913), which means in those souls which are capable of being active in an artistic, creative manner, especially in the social area. This is the beginning of developing the consciousness soul in the direction of Spirit Self, which is in the direction of the sixth epoch. The consciousness soul, as already mentioned, is absolutely individual in its nature and thereby bears within itself a certain inclination toward antisocial development. It strives continually for situations in which everyone cares only for himself alone. Thus, extreme individualization and increasing isolation are the most important accompanying symptoms of conscious soul development. The sixth epoch or epoch of the Spirit Self on the other hand will be a social one (see GA 186, 7 December 1918). Isn't the entire significance of the anthroposophical world society founded on this goal as long as we are prepared to turn to it earnestly enough?

We can only prepare the coming epoch of the Spirit Self together in a social sense. Such a social activity—in order to suffice the character of the consciousness soul—must precede intensive, individual cognitive work. Then its fruits must truly be realized in the social sphere, in which it is qualified to form the basis for the first seeds of the Spirit Self, which must be prepared beginning in our time. For this we need the General Anthroposophical Society with all of its different groups and branches, which unite all anthroposophists in the world, because the spiritual-social tasks laid on us can only be achieved through mutual efforts with one another.

A comprehensive spiritual brotherhood, which draws its inner forces from the common Spirit to prepare for the Spirit Self, must come from the Anthroposophical Society. 'Thereby we may imagine that we unite ourselves into brotherly study groups; invisible above our work hovers that which is like the child of those Spirit Self forces cared for by the beings of the higher hierarchies, so that it can stream down into our souls when they are here again in the sixth cultural epoch. In our brotherly study groups we accomplish work which streams upwards to the forces being prepared for the Spirit Self' (GA 159/160, 15 June 1915).

In Russian there is a special word for this future ideal, *Sobornost*,[8] which even in Russia is not correctly understood today. If we try to understand it with the help of anthroposophy, it becomes clear that as the most important goal of the sixth cultural epoch the building of a future social temple on earth can only be realized through individual efforts of people, who thanks to being penetrated by the unifying Spirit, the common Spirit of the 'inverted' Whitsun, have freely come together, built a new social community and are working out of it.

Rudolf Steiner connects this directly to the inner task of true Rosicrucianism, which saw the building of a social temple as its most important task. In the same sense Rudolf Steiner understands the merger of the single branches in the Anthroposophical Society.

At the foundation of the Neuchâtel branch he said, 'May the branch be a building stone for the temple we want to construct' (GA 180, 28 September 1911).

In 1923, while preparing the coming Christmas Conference, Rudolf Steiner spoke about the 'inverted cult' as spiritual foundation of each branch's activity. This should be 'celebrated' in the branch's soul-spiritual room in order to lead people into the realm of the hierarchies. In this social cult the angels will not descend to man, but people must learn to rise into the sphere of the angels (see GA 257, 3 March 1923).[9] This is that sphere of the spiritual world in which today the etheric Christ appears in an angel's garment (see GA 182, 2 May 1918).

Thus, regarding the coming sixth cultural epoch the spiritual tasks of the General Anthroposophical Society are gradually combined with the tasks of all mankind.

2. The Foundation Stone of the Christmas Conference and the Inverted Cult*

Individual and Social Life

The esoteric kernel of the Christmas Conference in 1923/24 is 'laying the foundation stone of the General Anthroposophical Society by Dr Rudolf Steiner', as it was announced in the conference programme for 25 December 1923, 10.00 a.m. In the accompanying text was added: 'On Tuesday, 25 December, when Rudolf Steiner lays the foundation stone, the General Anthroposophical Society will be consecrated' (GA 260, p. 28).[10] With the word 'consecration' Rudolf Steiner pointed out that it was not solely a matter of conveying wisdom (which happened during the Christmas Conference especially in the evening lectures), but a ritual act of the highest rank.

When we now turn to the text of laying the foundation stone, as it remains preserved in stenography, we can experience it as a quite unique *esoteric lesson* held by Rudolf Steiner for the members of the Anthroposophical Society. This began at first like his other esoteric lessons with direct communications from the spiritual world and proceeded to a simple description of what Rudolf Steiner, the leading initiate of our time, realized himself in this moment as a creative deed out of freedom and love in the spiritual world adjacent to the earth. He called this quite new creation brought forth by him a 'dodecahedral foundation stone of love', which he immediately thereafter presented to the newly founded Anthroposophical Society as its spiritual foundation.

We want to point out here a quite special characteristic of this foundation stone. It bears the force to connect continually the individual and social together, quite in the sense of the New Mysteries. For planting the foundation stone in the depth of the

---
* The phrase 'inverted cult' is also translatable as 'reverse ritual' or 'reverse cultus'. (Editor's note.)

human heart can only be realized by the individual himself as his free deed. When this is once anchored there it no longer works alone in the sense of individual spiritual development, but becomes an imperturbable fundament of a new human community.

Also in the Foundation Stone Meditation, which creates in its mantric form a type of spiritual-etheric garment or protective cover in the human heart, one can recognize a similar gesture. It begins with the threefold, strongly individual call 'Human soul', which Rudolf Steiner says refers to the 'human soul calling itself' (GA 260, 26 December 1923) and ends in a powerful 'we' chord, which testifies to the emergence of a new human community.

'That will be good
What we ...'

The entire act on 25 December of laying the foundation stone in its double form—the foundation stone itself and the Foundation Stone Meditation describing it—is related in its being, which Rudolf Steiner while preparing the Christmas Conference during 1923 represented as *inverted cult* (see GA 257). This cult was to be the most important source of community-building forces for that general anthroposophical work in branches and groups worldwide and therewith the basis for the new foundation of the Anthroposophical Society, which occurred at the Christmas Conference.

In connection with these two events we come to the question: how is the inverted cult connected with laying the foundation stone of the General Anthroposophical Society? An attempt will be made to answer it in what follows.

Building Stones of the Inverted Cult

First we want to turn to the being of the inverted cult itself. It consists of 'awakening a person to the spirit-soul of another person' (GA 257, 27 February 1923). As one awakens in the morning to ordinary daily consciousness, the possibility is predisposed in the inverted cult to raise oneself from this to a higher and therefore community-building consciousness soul condition.

Human daily consciousness is normally permeated primarily by thought life. For in the human soul this possesses the degree of awareness necessary for clear consciousness. The next higher stage to which a person can consciously ascend consists of consciously living fully in imaginations.[11] These play a decisive role for the social life of people among one another. Rudolf Steiner never tires of emphasizing that all social questions of mankind can be solved not with head thinking but only with imaginative consciousness. Therefore, as we will see, the capability developed by people to live in imaginations is of decisive importance for forming a spiritual-social order as well as realizing the inverted cult.

By occupying oneself with the question about the inverted cult it is often disregarded that this cannot develop in empty space, but requires a certain soul quality as starting point. Rudolf Steiner calls it 'spiritual idealism'. Without such a foundation the inverted cult awakening to the spirit-soul of other people cannot be realized. 'The strength for this awakening can be generated by planting spiritual idealism in a human community' (ibid.). In another place Rudolf Steiner gives a still more detailed account of what is concerned. Here it is not a matter of the commonly known 'innate' idealism, which more or less all young people bear in themselves and which gradually fades in the further course of life, but a new, consciously instilled idealism that never leaves the person who raises himself consciously to its heights, because he bears in our time a profound Christian foundation in himself. Therefore Rudolf Steiner brings this into connection with the modern human path on which Christ can be attained through inwardly unfolding will forces: 'Only in instilled idealism is realized what Paul's words about Christ mean to say: "Not I, but the Christ in me"' (GA 193, 11 February 1919).

Rudolf Steiner characterizes this 'spiritual idealism' further as a soul capability in a position to raise 'to ideal' through one's own free will all that a person has 'perceived in the world of senses'. Thereby in an inner process 'the sensible is raised to the supersensible', which is a process opposite to that of a sacramental cult in which 'the supersensible begins to be present sensibly in the altar substances' (GA 257, 27 February 1923).

The next step in caring for spiritual idealism occurs, according to Rudolf Steiner, through what he calls the force of 'enthusiasm', which exists in the unfolding of feeling and will forces in people. Thereby, 'the ideal gains a higher life' (ibid.) and becomes henceforth capable of guiding the protected human soul into the spiritual world. For 'enthusiasm bears the spirit (*Geist*) in itself' (GA 260a, 20 July 1924), a fact to which the German word (*Begeisterung*) testifies. Enthusiasm means: 'to be in spirit'.

Then Rudolf Steiner adds yet a third characteristic, which along with spiritual idealism and the force of enthusiasm belongs inalienably to founding the inverted cult and even forms its breeding ground. That is the atmosphere to be cultivated mutually in branches and groups through activity with anthroposophical wisdom. Here it is a matter of consequent 'cultivation of spiritualized perception' which Rudolf Steiner also described with the word 'respect'. Only in such an atmosphere can the inverted cult really prosper in anthroposophical branches and groups. 'We can achieve that in an emotional way when we make it our business wherever we cultivate anthroposophy to maintain this spiritualized perception, when we understand the doors and gateways to the room—may it be ever so profane, it will be hallowed through anthroposophical group lectures[12]—as something sensed which we metamorphose with *respect*' (GA 257, 27 February 1923).

Also after the Christmas Conference he writes about '*respect* for spiritual life' (on 23 March 1924 in the tenth letter to members, GA 260a; italics Rudolf Steiner), which must be at work in the branches 'in complete anthroposophical representation'. For 'where this respect is missing, there is no strength in discussing anthroposophical truths' (ibid.). This inner strength is necessary so the higher beings can unite with anthroposophical work in the branches.

One can perhaps ask why just *this* atmosphere is of such special importance in branch life. The answer is: due to the goal of anthroposophical group work in connection with spiritual beings. That cannot be accomplished without this atmosphere, which is why it can also be called a real threshold atmosphere.

On the contrary, it often has a depressing effect, when just this inner condition of the inverted cult is disregarded in group branch work, whereby this sooner or later falls into decay. Here it should be especially emphasized that Rudolf Steiner's above-mentioned words do not represent a citation from 'old theosophical times', but the life conditions of an Anthroposophical Society which was prepared gradually by the initiate at the forthcoming founding of the New Mysteries at the Christmas Conference in 1923/1924. Even later these basic conditions for the progress of anthroposophical branch work were continually expressed by him.

Thus, it is not surprising that Rudolf Steiner right in his opening talk at the Christmas Conference said with great emphasis that what participants should bring especially to this conference is 'atmosphere, atmosphere, and once again atmosphere' (GA 260, 24 December 1923). Along with this 'anthroposophical atmosphere' (ibid.) he also mentions 'enthusiasm' which this conference needed in order to attain its goal. Thereby the essential characteristics of the inverted cult are directly incorporated in the Christmas Conference event.

Cooperation of Spiritual Beings

In this connection one may have no illusions: where in branches and groups a respectful atmosphere is not sufficiently and consequently cultivated there exists no inverted cult. For in the end it has the task of leading its participants to the goal 'that through the entire process of receiving anthroposophical ideas a real spiritual being becomes present in the room in which we conduct anthroposophy' (GA 257, 27 February 1923). Only when this stage of group work is attained 'the specific anthroposophical effectiveness starts to realize the supersensible itself' (ibid.). Then in a branch one begins to speak not about, but out of anthroposophy. Now a being from the realm of higher hierarchies can unite with such an anthroposophical group or such a branch as the new group spirit or the new group soul. (In other places this theme has been presented in more detail.[13])

In the New Mysteries such cooperation occurs not only because higher beings descend but also while the opposite movement is possible: ascent of people into the spiritual world through the inverted cult. According to Rudolf Steiner therein lies the true goal of branch work. 'The work of an anthroposophical group does not exist simply because a number of people talk about anthroposophical ideas, but as people they feel so united, their human souls awaken to one another and people are transplanted to the spiritual world—so they are really among spiritual beings, even though these cannot be seen' (GA 257, 3 March 1923).

When the inverted cult continues to unfold in anthroposophical groups under the stated conditions, then already in our time even though at first only in initial stages, the task is fulfilled which Rudolf Steiner expresses in the following words: 'People must work together with the gods, with Michael himself' (GA 240, 19 July 1924).

Four Stages of the Inverted Cult

Referring to the formation of human community and the new group souls connected with this process, Rudolf Steiner says: 'Through what we experience by absorbing anthroposophy in groups, rather than a group spirit through the blood (like the old group souls), a real community spirit is invoked. If we are able to feel this, then we bind ourselves together as people to true community' (GA 257, 27 February 1923). In another lecture he describes this 'invoked' real community spirit as a being who initially belongs to the angel hierarchy. This means that not through external forms of cooperation, but especially through the mutual search for being together with hierarchical beings, real anthroposophical group work can eventually work healthily and productively in a social sense in the world. Practising the inverted cult is the concrete path thereto (see ibid.).

If one looks closer at the stages inherent in the cult, through which a new human community cooperating consciously with the spiritual world comes about, then the following development can be identified. First one proceeds from the foundation of spiritual idealism, which can be understood in the sense of the well-known statement from *Knowledge of the Higher Worlds and Its Attainment*: 'Every idea that does not become ideal destroys a force in your soul; every idea that does become an ideal creates life force in you' (GA 10, p. 28). The goal of unfolding this idealism in social life is forming a human community founded on pure brotherly love.

Between the starting point of this path and attaining the goal lies however a decisive intermediate stage, which leads directly to the social being. This intermediate stage consists of forming imaginations. For the social question can, as already mentioned above, never be solved by the loftiest ideals as long as they remain only intellectual, but solely by creating new imaginations. For only these are able to call into life and maintain such a human community in which true brotherhood founded on love can blossom. For this reason Rudolf Steiner points out in paragraph 3 of the Christmas Conference statutes that the results of anthroposophy maintained at the Goetheanum can lead 'to a real social life built on brotherly love' (GA 260a, 13 January 1924).

Solely in such human communities founded on brotherly love in which through occupation with anthroposophy not only thoughts but especially participants' feelings flow together as into an invisible centre, a real connection with the spiritual world and its inherent spiritual beings as a new group soul is possible. 'Inasmuch as people voluntarily allow their feelings to radiate together, something beyond simply emancipated people will be formed ... On the other hand, the feelings flowing to a midpoint give cause for [spiritual] beings to work like a type of group soul' (GA 102, 1 June 1908). Thereby especially the streaming together of all participants' feelings into a common 'midpoint' in such anthroposophical work is of great importance. However, this must first be formed in the appropriate manner from the anthroposophical content in which all are really enthused. For the spiritual work binding all participants internally produces the 'community feeling' which attracts higher beings (new group souls). 'And the more community feelings are developed out of full freedom the more sublime [spiritual] beings will descend to people' (ibid.).

In this early Rudolf Steiner lecture, he points to the new group souls that want to cooperate today with the person becoming free in social life. In my opinion it is a matter of the same 'group souls or group spirits' about which he spoke in 1923 in connection with the inverted cult. Rudolf Steiner describes the conscious connection with it as a new 'community with the Spirit', which in a spiritual sense can work alone today forming community. For wherever people in their awakened souls 'receive anthroposophical ideas, the common real spirit descends upon their place of work' (GA 257, 27 February 1923) so that 'spirits in spiritual gathering [anthroposophy] can have spiritual community with us' (ibid.). In summarizing the entire process he says: 'If this true understanding for anthroposophy is there, this understanding is not only the path to ideas of spirits but to community with the spirits. Consciousness of this community with the spiritual world also forms community' (ibid.).

There can arise on earth new communities of brotherly love in which people on the path of the inverted cult ascend into the spiritual world and the hierarchical beings come towards them from above, where a new manner of meeting and working is possible between gods and people. On this basis, the following four stages can be differentiated in the inverted cult:

Grasping anthroposophical ideas in the sense of spiritual idealism so they become a source of mutual enthusiasm and thereby awaken interest in the thoughts of other people.

Developing the capability of experiencing other people pictorially or imaginatively, as Rudolf Steiner described particularly in the lecture of 26 October 1918. 'That will be what in this age of the consciousness soul must come upon mankind: being able to understand people pictorially' for 'we must learn to see through the spiritual prototype of a person, through his pictorial nature' (GA 185). This new capability leads then to the real awakening of the soul to the spirit-soul of the other person. After the Christmas Conference, the thirteenth letter to members dated 18 May 1924, to which Marie Steiner gave the title 'The Pictorial Nature of People',[14] points to the same task. In the article 'What is Revealed When One Looks Back on the Previous Life Between Death and New Birth?' (December 1924) Rudolf Steiner adds that the 'human form ... is spiritual through and through' and 'he who has spiritual sight sees in the human form a real imagination that has descended to the physical world' (GA 26).

Forming a new human community out of brotherly love which has as its central task the cultivation of anthroposophical wisdom in groups and gradually forms in its spiritual work the above-mentioned 'midpoint' in which participants' higher feelings flow together so that a soul-spirit sheath develops for the presence of hierarchical beings.[15]

Experiencing the 'community of the Spirit' in such anthroposophical human connection through the presence of angelic or even higher group souls.

Activity of the Angel in the Astral Body

In the lecture of 9 October 1918 with the title 'What Does the Angel Do in Our Astral Body?' Rudolf Steiner describes how in our time the spiritual beings from the angel hierarchy give rise in the human astral body to images (imaginations) that have the task of calling forth three future ideals in the human soul.

The first ideal is characterized as a 'true brotherly impulse,' as 'correctly understood brotherhood referring to social conditions in the physical life' (GA 182).

The second ideal to which the above-mentioned images of the angel lead is 'that in the future each person should see in every person a concealed divine being' (ibid.). In order to attain this goal it is however necessary 'to understand a person *as image* that is revealed from the spiritual world' (ibid.). Especially impressive are the results of such pictorial and/or imaginative understanding of the other person for the social form of living together. For out of it unfolds with time a 'free religiosity' which means that in social life 'the meeting of each person with every person becomes from the start a religious action, a sacrament'. Thereby the entire life of a person on the physical plane is 'an expression of the supersensible'.

The third ideal consists of realizing the step that is stimulated through the images called forth by the angel in the human astral body: 'To arrive at spirit through thinking' (ibid.), that is, to come to an understanding of modern *spiritual science*.

'Spiritual science for the spirit, religious freedom for the soul, brotherhood for the bodies, that sounds like world music through the work of the angels in the human astral body'—with these words Rudolf Steiner summarizes the three capabilities described.

Then he describes as the most important task of the present: that a person gradually should become conscious of the angel's activity in his astral body, should even be able to see the angel itself. 'People must come to this purely through their consciousness soul, through their conscious thinking so they *see* what the angel does in order to prepare mankind's future' (ibid.).

If we remember here that within the third hierarchy the angels, with a completely developed Spirit Self, represent above all the impulse of the Holy Ghost (see GA 175, 20 February 1917) and as such can be experienced on the path of modern initiation, then we also find here the well-known four stages of the inverted cult.

Thus, the three basic characteristics to which the angel wants to lead people through images called forth in their soul consists of:

Studying spiritual science.

Experiencing other people in images.[16]

Attaining true brotherhood in social life.

Added to these is the fourth stage of consciously meeting with the angel as man's next higher representative of spirit who plays at the same time a mediating role between it and the higher hierarchies (archangels and archai).

As in the inverted cult it is a matter primarily of *awakening* a person in his consciousness soul for the next higher stage of world being on which he can really be among the angels, so it is also with reference to the activity of the angel in the astral body—in order to fulfil the future ideal of the sixth cultural epoch, especially in the area of community building.[17]

Inverted Cult and the Foundation Stone

The same four stages that we have recognized as belonging to the inverted cult are also found in the being of the Christmas Conference's foundation stone:

It receives its aura out of *World-Human-Thoughts*, which mutually becomes an ideal, because the human thoughts unite themselves here with world thoughts.

Its form consists of *World-Human-Imaginations* through which one understands the higher being of another person, because human imaginations are connected to world imaginations and make a person's spiritual being perceptible.

Its substance consists of *World-Human-Love*, which is in a position to found a new human community. For now individual human love is connected with world love and thereby works in a social forming way.

Finally, as culmination of this whole process, there appears on the fourth stage in the thought aura of the foundation stone, corresponding in the inverted cult to the study of anthroposophy in groups, *the Spirit* whose representative in the supersensible world is the angelic or still higher group soul which descends on the group.

In the process of laying the foundation stone, Rudolf Steiner added the corresponding tasks that must be fulfilled by a person so that in the sense of the inverted cult the foundation stone can become effective in one's own heart.

Referring to the imaginative form connected with the heart as core of the central system Rudolf Steiner formulated the task of activating 'the heart as cognitive organ' which is then capable of perceiving 'world images', that is, cosmic imaginations. For in contrast to the head the heart does not understand in thoughts, but in imaginations.

In connection with the foundation stone's substance, which is inwardly connected with the spiritual basis of a person's limb system, Rudolf Steiner speaks about the task of fulfilling one's 'duties, tasks and mission in the world' (GA 260, 25 December 1923), that is, understanding consciously one's karma as it lives and works in the circulation-limb system and realizing it in a human community. For karma acts among people. Therefore, Rudolf Steiner answered the question about what unites people in the Anthroposophical Society: 'What unites them is they should bring their karma in order!' (GA 237, 8 August 1924).

The Spirit itself, which appeared during the laying of the foundation stone in the thought aura of the love stone, becomes at the end of the Christmas Conference the 'good star' which wants to lead the newly founded community of anthroposophists through its divine light into the future (see GA 260, 1 January 1924).

From all this it follows that the four components of the foundation stone correspond precisely to the above-mentioned stages of the inverted cult. Thus, planting it in the ground of one's own heart leads also to realizing the inverted cult. In this manner the inverted cult becomes integrated in the Christmas Conference mystery event and thereby the foundation for the entire esoteric life of the Anthroposophical Society.

Cultivating the Inverted Cult in a Branch

An important component of Anthroposophical Society esotericism forms the inner life of the branch. Therefore, after the Christmas

Conference Rudolf Steiner devoted to this theme several 'Letters to Members'. It is meaningful that in the fifteenth letter to members, dated 6 January 1924, with the title 'More About the Necessary Atmosphere of Branch Gatherings', he characterized the four stages mentioned above although from a somewhat different viewpoint (GA 260a). This renewed return to the theme proceeds from the observation that anthroposophy in no way makes people naive, but its higher interpretation can increase proficiency in the world.

Furthermore, the following stages are also found in the letter. The first stage: 'Filling the internal human with knowledge of the spirit is an *awakening* out of life into sensible reality' (ibid.). Here it is a matter of a person's inner awakening leading beyond the borders of daily consciousness, which is similar to that of the inverted cult. In both cases it is initially a matter of (knowledge-based) intellect contending with anthroposophical content.

The second stage is described in the following way: 'Life in material existence is for a person that stage in which the spiritual outside of its reality can be perceived *as an image*' (ibid., italics Rudolf Steiner). Here it concerns the development of a new, imaginative capability with which the pictorial nature of a person also can be grasped. This experience augments still further the process of a person's inner awakening, which previously had begun through the study of anthroposophy in groups.

In the preceding, fourteenth letter Rudolf Steiner pointed out that such imaginative observation of a person's 'pictorial being' leads to one's inner 'awakening' (GA 260a, 25 May 1924) through the necessary special soul attitude alone. If one asks about the source of this awakening, he finds it in the sense of the inverted cult, in the spirit-soul of another person, which is experienced by intensifying his pictorial nature.

Based on this imaginative perception, through which the inner being of a person gradually becomes visible, interest and real devotion to the other person blossom in social life. Rudolf Steiner writes further: 'In this devotion lies the foundation of the love impulse in life' (fifteenth letter). Thus, the brotherly togetherness of people among one another actually becomes possible, which represents the third stage of the path described.

Finally, Rudolf Steiner mentions in the same letter also the *Spirit* which 'true anthroposophy' seeks everywhere in nature and which in this culminating fourth stage can appear and be active in branch gatherings when in them the 'right atmosphere' resulting from the three previous stages is consciously cultivated. Only then will branch work be capable in the sense of the inverted cult to give to a person what he needs for his life in the external world. 'The Spirit that works in branch gatherings must become light that continues to shine when a member is faced with the external demands of the day.' Therefore, it will emanate from the spiritual light, about which Rudolf Steiner spoke twice during the Christmas Conference after laying the foundation stone (25 December 1923) and on the last day (1 January 1924).

From this we can see that Rudolf Steiner, although he neither at the Christmas Conference nor thereafter mentioned the inverted cult *expressis verbis*, connected the entire laying of the foundation stone as the esoteric midpoint of the same with this cult and apparently also planned to unfold the being of branch work out of the inverted cult with its four stages in the sense of the fifteenth letter to members. Thus the inverted cult remains inseparably connected with the foundation stone and works further in a mysterious way in the branches when they maintain the new 'esoteric trend' which proceeded from the Christmas Conference, and intend to work in this sense.

If we are able to stand imperturbably on this spiritual foundation stone in all of our anthroposophical work, in all internal and external situations, then we may be active with our initiatives in the world as much as possible. Based on its presence in our hearts we will never run into danger of losing the necessary relationship to our spiritual roots in anthroposophy. Conversely, should we be in danger of occupying ourselves too strongly with ourselves and losing sight of anthroposophy's essential goals, then it will once again be the foundation stone that like an inner admonisher, through its innate community-building force, will bring us back to the current tasks of mankind. For 'the right ground in which we must lay the current foundation stone, the right ground being our hearts in their harmonic interplay, in their good love-penetrated will, can bear the anthroposophical intention through the world together. It will be able to radiate admonishingly towards us out of the thought light that can at any time stream towards us from the dodecahedral stone of love, which we want today to sink into our hearts' (GA 260, 25 December 1923).

Thus, in the foundation stone there are contained from the beginning two poles inseparably connected in full harmony with another: in one's thought-light the individual is active, in one's love-substance the social. Its imaginative form however unites in full freedom both these poles and allows a new human community as the Anthroposophical Society to come about and flourish in which the multiple initiatives of the real Spirit can be present and effective for the progress of mankind.

Notes

1. 'The book contains the outlines of anthroposophy as a whole' (GA 13, p. 31).
2. See S.O. Prokofieff, *Rudolf Steiner and the Founding of the New Mysteries*, London 1994; *May Human Beings Hear It! The Mystery of the Christmas Conference*, Sussex 2004; *The Foundation Stone Meditation. A Key to the Christian Mysteries*, Sussex 2006; F. Willem Zeylmans van Emmichoven, *The Foundation Stone*, Sussex 2002; Rudolf Grosse, *The Christmas Conference: Beginning of a New Age*, Victoria 1984; B.C.J. Lievegoed, *Mystery Streams in Europe and the New Mysteries*, London 1982.
3. See GA 130, 1 October 1911 and Peter Selg, *Mysterium Cordis: Von der Mysterienstätte des Menschenherzens*, Dornach 2003.
4. Up to here the translation from Russian into German stems from Dr Julia Selg. Further text was translated from Russian into German by Anna S. Fischer.
5. See S.O. Prokofieff, 'Eurythmie als christliche Kunst. Vom Ursprungsimpuls und Wesen des Eurythmischen, in: *Eurythmie. Ein kosmischer Impuls durch Rudolf Steiner*, Günther von Negelein, Dornach 2007.
6. See S.O. Prokofieff, *The East in the Light of the West, Parts One to Three*, Sussex 2009.
7. See more detail in the second part of this book, pp. 30–43.
8. *Sobor* in Russian means both cathedral and human gathering: a human community, namely one formed by people as a soul-spirit temple so that social life can be penetrated by higher beings of the spiritual world.
9. See also S.O. Prokofieff, *The Esoteric Significance of Spiritual Work in Anthroposophical Groups and the Future of the Anthroposophical Society*, Sussex 2007.
10. In both citations from the conference programme Rudolf Steiner used the term 'International Anthroposophical Society' which he later, during the conference, requested not to be used any more but to replace it with the word 'General' (see opening lecture on 24 December 1923). Citations here and following are from GA 260, 1985.

11. See *Stages of Higher Knowledge* (GA 12).
12. In the same lecture Rudolf Steiner speaks in a similar sense about other forms 'of taking up anthroposophical ideas' in branches. Thus he also mentions along with reading in groups 'what's heard', that is, lectures held as well as independent elaboration of anthroposophical contents.
13. S.O. Prokofieff, *The Esoteric Significance of Spiritual Work in Anthroposophical Groups and the Future of the Anthroposophical Society*, Sussex 2007.
14. It is also significant that letters to members appear thematically in this order: first the twelfth letter 'The Formation of Branch Evenings', then the thirteenth mentioned 'The Pictorial Nature of People', and then one with the title 'The Atmosphere Needed in Branch Gatherings' (fourteenth letter).
15. In these first three stages of the inverted cult it is easy to recognize the threefold ideal of the true Rosicrucians, which combines science, art, and religion (social life).
16. It is of special importance that in the same lecture Rudolf Steiner particularly brings this central characteristic in connection with perceiving Christ in the etheric.
17. It is not difficult, in the three characteristics that proceed from images of the angels, to recognize the three main aspects of the sixth cultural epoch (see in regard to the latter GA 159/160, 15 June 1915).

Bibliography

The bibliographical numbers ('GA') correspond to the series of volumes of Rudolf Steiner's complete works published by the Rudolf Steiner Nachlassverwaltung in Dornach, Switzerland. In the following list, titles of the comparable English publications containing the relevant lectures are given where relevant.

All italics in quotations derive from the present author, unless stated otherwise.

GA

Books and Articles

4	*The Philosophy of Spiritual Activity / The Philosophy of Freedom*
10	*Knowledge of the Higher Worlds*
11	*Cosmic Memory*
12	*Stages of Higher Knowledge*
13	*Occult Science, An Outline*
26	*Anthroposophical Leading Thoughts*
28	*Autobiography*

Lectures

100	*Menschheitsentwickelung und Christus-Erkenntnis*
102	*The Influence of Spiritual Beings Upon Man*
104	*The Apocalypse of St John*
118	*Das Ereignis der Christus-Erscheinung in der ätherischen Welt*
130	*Esoteric Christianity and the Mission of Christian Rosenkreuz*
131	*From Jesus to Christ*
145	*The Effects of Spiritual Development*
148	*The Fifth Gospel*
159/160	*Das Geheimnis des Todes*
175	*Cosmic and Human Metamorphoses*
180	*Ancient Myths*
182	*Der Tod als Lebenswandlung*
185	*From Symptom to Reality in Modern History*
186	*Die soziale Grundforderung unserer Zeit—In geänderter Zeitlage*
193	*Der innere Aspekt des sozialen Rätsels*

212	*Human Soul in Relation to World Evolution*
214	*The Mystery of the Trinity*
237	*Karmic Relationships, vol. 3*
240	*Karmic Relationships, vols 6 and 8*
257	*Awakening to Community*
260	*The Christmas Conference Proceedings*
260a	*Die Konstitution der Allgemeinen Anthroposophischen Gesellschaft und der Freien Hochschule für Geisteswissenschaft*

Works by Rudolf Steiner are available via Rudolf Steiner Press, UK (www.rudolfsteinerpress.com) or SteinerBooks, USA (www.steinerbooks.org).